Power Moves:

How We Went From Over $1,000,000 in Debt to Debt-Free in 24 Months!

By

Twa'Lea A. Jordan and Andre Jordan

AF808355

This book is dedicated to:

Azalea, Zaya, and Zayden. May the stones we've laid always serve as a memorial to how good God is and how much He loves you.

Copyright © 2019 JordanGirls Publishing – All rights reserved. No part of this publication may be reproduced, stored in a retrieval system or transmitted, in any form, or by any means, electronic, mechanical, recorded, photocopied, or otherwise reproduced without the prior express written authorization of JordanGirls Publishing, except by a reviewer who may quote brief passages in a review.

Cover Photo Credit: XTG Media

Table of Contents

Introduction

In a matter of twenty-four months, we went from being over a million dollars in debt to being completely debt free. This book will tell you how we found ourselves in over a million dollars in debt, and what we did to eradicate that debt. Neither one of us is a financial expert. We just knew that we wanted to live extraordinary lives before our children. We knew that we wanted to live out biblical financial principles before them. We knew that we wanted to leave them an inheritance.

This is not a "self-help" book. This is a "tell-all" book. We take turns writing the chapters. In this book, we will share our journey, and we pray that it is inspirational and encouraging to you. We will detail what our journey to becoming debt free looked and felt like. If you are on the journey to becoming debt free, maybe seeing some commonalities will be helpful to know that what you are feeling is "normal". If you desire to become debt free but you don't know where to start, maybe something you read in this book will resonate with you. If you don't believe being debt free is possible, maybe this book will change your mind.

We like hearing success stories. There is something to be said about a great success story. The success is "catching". We believe that is why the Bible is full of stories about overcoming and conquest. That is why some people like reading autobiographies and biographies. When we read these stories, we can imagine ourselves conquering too. That is what we hope will happen when you read our story. This is a story about overcoming and conquering. If we can do it, so can you!

Chapter One: The Catalyst

The rich rule over the poor, and the borrower is a slave to the lender. ***Proverbs* 22:7**

Debt. That is what got us where we are today. There is no pretty word to describe debt. There is no eloquent way of describing debt. Some may want to know, "Why would you worry about being in debt if you weren't behind in your payments?" That is a great question!

When we embarked on the journey of eliminating our debts, we were both working full-time and Andre was serving in the Air Force Reserves. We had just purchased our second home. We had a rental property, two vehicles, and "three whole kids". We had plenty of savings in the bank and plenty of food in the fridge. A few months prior we had traveled to Cape Town, South Africa, as a family. We were not looking to "bankrupt" ourselves, or drastically change our lives, but little did we know that God was looking to take us on a journey.

In March of 2017, right after our son was born, Andre was sent on military duty to Wichita Falls, Texas. While he was gone, I started feeling like we needed to make some changes in our finances. I evaluated our student loan debts and for the first time, I realized how they were a form of mental bondage for me. I learned that my loans alone were gaining over a thousand dollars in interest per month. I felt overwhelmed by the debt. It felt like modern day indentured servitude. Although we had hoped to obtain student

loan forgiveness after ten years, ten years felt like an eternity. I considered the thought that if something were to happen to either

Andre or me, the student loan companies would come and take any assets we had to pay off the debts. I felt hopeless and powerless about the odds of the student loans being paid off. The feelings became overwhelming.

I began to pray about how I was feeling. I asked God to send me direction and to order my steps. One day, our new neighbors invited me over so they could meet our son. I remember sitting in their chair while they held our son. I started sharing with them the feelings I had regarding our student loans. I did not discuss numbers, but I shared how I really wanted to start attacking the debt. I did not know these people personally. They did not know me. Why would I be telling them about my family's finances? Because God was about to use them to change my family's path in life.

While I sat in my neighbors' chair sharing the concerns of my heart, they gave me a book, "The Total Money Makeover" by Dave Ramsey. My initial thought was, "Where am I going to find the time to myself to read this book?" Andre was away on military duty, and I had "three whole kids" to look after. I put the book on my nightstand and walked past it a few times over the next couple of days. When the weekend came, I took it with me when I when to the nail salon to get a pedicure. My thought was, "I may not get to finish this book, but I should at least start it, so that if I run into my neighbor, and he asks me about it, I can tell him that I started it." Unbeknownst to me, when I started reading the book, I just couldn't stop.

After reading Ramsey's book I felt empowered about tackling our debt. I was excited, and I wanted to get started. I began sharing the information I obtained with Andre while he was away. I began praying and fasting about God's direction and plan. For the first time since graduating from law school, I felt optimistic about eliminating our student loan debt. I was more excited about tackling our student loans than I was about the possibility of student loan forgiveness. I felt that us making the decision to annihilate our student loans put the power in our hands rather than us being at the mercy of who held governmental office over the course of ten faithful years of public service. I felt that us making the decision to eradicate our student loans would speed up our "release from bondage" date.

Simultaneous to God dealing with me regarding our student loans, God was dealing with our church's leadership regarding the financial matters of our church. Our church launched a three-year campaign with the goal of eliminating debt, funding the church's mission, and taking care of matters of the church's building, set to conclude in 2020. Our church asked the members to pray about making a campaign contribution to help with the church's financial goals.

When we heard about the church's campaign we knew that we were headed in the right direction. Things were aligning and we made a choice to get in alignment with the direction that God was leading the ministry. We made a sacrificial financial pledge to support the church's campaign. We stood in agreement that as God took care of His house, He would also take care of our house. As God was leading the church out of debt, that he would do the same for our family. We set our sights on being debt free in 2020. We didn't know how God was going to do it, but we trusted that He would.

We gave a sacrificial gift of $2,500 to our church's campaign. Then, we took a good hard look at our finances and got to work.

What We Learned

Don't be afraid to be transparent about your struggles because you never know how God might use them to throw you a life preserver. Transparency is a breeding ground for new ideas, confidence, and inspiration.

Chapter Two: A Lean, Mean, No Extra Spending Machine

The plans of the diligent lead surely to abundance, but everyone who is hasty comes only to poverty. **Proverbs 21:5**

After we set our minds to slay our debt, we had to go through our budget and make some changes. We have always been good at making and following a family budget, so making one wasn't our issue. We didn't like to waste money and we liked to know what was coming in and what was going out. We had also gotten rid of cable television back in 2014, so there wasn't much to trim off the budget as far as unnecessary bills. What we needed to adjust was what we did with our dispensable income.

Our previous budget consisted of paying our tithes and offerings, paying our bills, setting money aside for gas and food, saving at least twenty percent of our income, and then giving ourselves individual allowances to splurge throughout the month. Our splurge money was our splurge money. We could spend it without dedicating any brain cells to it if we wanted to. If I wanted to spend it all at Macy's, I could. If I wanted to take a girls trip to Los Angeles for the day I could. However, when that money was gone for the month, it was gone and there was no dipping into other pots of money.

Our new budget included redirecting all of that splurge money to debt. It took discipline and focus. It was probably more challenging for me than it was for Andre. I really like to shop. I do not like to overpay for things, but I like the idea of being able to browse through stores and find good deals. Shopping is therapy for me. I could spend hours strolling through Marshalls looking for something that I might need later. I would look forward to my Macy's coupons coming in the mail so I could make my way to the store, grab a sale item, and slap a coupon on it. Needless to say, giving up my dispensable income, in and of itself, was a sacrifice for me.

I went through my emails and unsubscribed from all my store solicitation emails. I did not need the temptation. I committed to buying any "new" clothes from thrift stores. This meant new clothes for the kids AND me. No splurging on random kitchen or household items.

As for Andre, he isn't a big spender. The sacrifice that he made for the team was to take his lunch ritualistically. I cooked a great portion of our meals. Eating out was not in the budget. Thus, I would make enough dinner to make sure that there was enough left over for lunch the next day for the whole family. This was a sacrifice for Andre because he is a social person at work. When people at work would invite him to lunch, he would take time before their lunch event to gobble down his homemade lunch, then he would go to lunch with them and order a tall glass of ice water with two lemon wedges. I would laugh when he would tell me his comical versions of those stories. We would laugh together with the common knowledge that, "this too would pass."

We made the commitment that there would be no big purchases or large trips until we reached our financial goal. The canceling of large trips was the absolute hardest. We had become accustomed to taking at least one international trip, and at least three other trips, throughout the year. Traveling is what we worked hard for. Traveling was what we looked forward to. It was so ingrained in our family's culture that our young kids came to expect it and they asked about travel destinations.

Another challenge we faced in setting our budget and sticking to it came when a family member came for us for financial assistance. We had to talk through the decision. I think it was more difficult for us to communicate our position than it was for us to make the decision. We knew that we had to be leering of getting off track from our goal, but sometimes the most difficult part of a decision-making process comes from how we feel others will perceive our choice. It wasn't our goal to hurt their feelings. We had to realize that we couldn't control their feelings. We had to set a boundary. We communicated our decision with love and prayed they understood.

Boundaries had to be set with our children as well. When it comes to my children, I am like putty in their hands. I love to see them smile, and I love to treat them to nice experiences. However, boundaries had to be set with our children, which limited the activities they were able to participate in. I homeschool my oldest daughter. One of the benefits of homeschooling is that most of her extracurricular activities are covered by her school budget. With my youngest daughter, however, we had to hustle up some extra cash to help her not feel deprived. One day we took our oldest daughter to her first school-sponsored swimming lesson. Our youngest sat on the sideline and cried because she wasn't able to swim. It was heartbreaking to know that had we not been "snowballing" our debt, our youngest daughter would be right in the pool taking lessons. This didn't sit well with me. We could not take away from our set budget, but I could put in some extra hours grinding in order to make sure we met our goal and pay for her swim lessons. That is exactly what I did.

What We Learned

Setting healthy boundaries, in addition to establishing and communicating clear expectations while pursuing goals, is vital to success. This is applicable in all areas of life.

Chapter Three: Cutting Up the Credit Cards

I will lift up my eyes unto the hills – but where does my help come from? My help comes from the Lord who made Heaven and Earth. ***Psalms 121:1-2***

A big part of what we did was making the decision to live a debt-free life. We were going to tackle the debt that we had accrued and we made a conscious decision not to incur any future debt. At the time that we started this journey we had a car note on one vehicle, two mortgages, and student loan debt. We will talk more in detail about these debts later. We had minimal credit card debt.

When Twa'Lea said, "Yeah, and we have to cut up the credit cards," I remember looking at her like she had lost her mind. Why would we cut up perfectly good credit cards? We were not abusers of credit. We were actually quite the opposite. We used them for purchasing items that we would usually purchase with cash so that we could get points and rewards. We paid our bills on time every month and, for the most part, we paid our balances off every month. If it wasn't broke, why did we need to fix it?

I have to be honest. The day we sat in the office and cut up our credit cards, I still wasn't convinced it was a great idea. We would be left without a safety net and without the comfort of a large credit card limit. We wouldn't be able to gather "valuable" points to put toward nice vacations. Macy's would probably stop sending Twa'Lea coupons and she might resort to paying full price for things. Either way, I went along with the actions because I'm always down to test and prove. I'm glad I did and this is why…

Credit cards helped us immediately satisfy our every desire. If there was something we wanted, we could just charge it. They made us feel wealthy and privileged. In fact, we were not wealthy. We could buy things immediately, but we were not wealthy. We were the opposite. We were in debt for over one million dollars. Let that sink in. We did not need to be buying ANYTHING immediately. We needed to be putting all of our energy into digging ourselves out of the hole that we were in.

Cutting up the credit cards helped us to solely rely on God for everything we needed. Every month that we made it without a financial crisis, we knew that it was God's grace that sustained us. Throughout our years of marriage we have experienced lay-offs and tax increases, but we knew that we would be fine because we had God, a six months cushion in our savings account, and, if all else failed, we had a $25,000 credit limit. Well, in this season, all we had was God and our $2,500 emergency fund. Our mortgage alone was more than our emergency fund. So in essence, all we truly had to sustain us was God. Being in that position strengthened our faith, and helped solidify that God was truly in charge of this experience.

What We Learned

Credit cards can give a false sense of wealth and financial stability. They provided the illusion that we were wealthy because we could buy whatever we wanted. We prefer to actually be wealthy and financially stable.

When we allowed God to be at the center of the financial decisions, we experienced greater faith and trust in Him and His Word.

Chapter Four: Walking in Faith

Now faith is the substance of things hoped for, the evidence of things not seen. ***Hebrews 11:1***

In March of 2017, when we embarked upon this journey toward financial freedom, essentially what we did was bankrupt ourselves. This is what we started with:

Debts	
Car Loan	$17,339
Student Loans	$303,892
Rental Property Mortgage	$190,485
Home Mortgage	$492,769
Total Debts	**$1,004,485.00**

We had what most people consider "good debt". None of it was revolving credit. None of it was payday loans. None of it was past due. However, there is no such thing as "good debt." All debt holds us back from living and giving regardless of the type and the amount. We had goals of being millionaires, but we owed a million. If we wanted to pick up and move to Timbuktu and live off the fruit of the land, we wouldn't be able to do that. We had shackles and an anchor around our ankles. We wanted to leave an inheritance for our children, however, in the situation we were in, any inheritance that we would leave to them would get usurped by our creditors.

When we decided to go down this path of eliminating our debt in record speed, we were both W-2 employees. A few months into it we decided that it would be best for our family for Twa'Lea to stay home with our children. That had always been a desire of hers and, with three children that were not school age, it seemed like a fiscally responsible decision to make. At the time Twa'Lea was working as a teacher. Her paycheck would have pretty much been paying for daycare. We took a leap of faith and prayed that other avenues of income would open up such as her legal clients and tutoring. She also had hopes of opening an in-home preschool program.

When we started, we had $17,197 dollars in savings. We took all of that and paid off our car. The immediate feeling of knocking down one of our debts was invigorating. It was sad to see all of that cash disappear, but it also empowered us. We eliminated our $400 car payment and then started throwing that money at our student loans. We started looking at more ways that we could acquire more money to throw at our loans. When I say throw, I mean it felt like we were angry and fed up with how our debt had us bound. Every time we made a payment it was like we were saying, "Here, take your money and scram!" So, yes, we were "throwing" money at our debt.

It took a huge leap of faith to deplete our cushion savings. That was our "just in case" money. That money was to protect us from unemployment, a broken washing machine, car break-downs, and any other emergency that could occur in any given month. Once we began to liquidate our accounts and put it towards our debts, it helped remove the false and misplaced sense of security we associated with our bank accounts. We were really "tightrope walking" this process, and operating on faith without our cushion savings and safety net. No more pretending that our faith was in God alone. It was now time to test how much we truly trusted God to supply all of our needs according to His riches and glory.

What We Learned

We had to have the confidence that the sacrificial decisions we make to better our financial affairs (and life for that matter) may not always be easy, but they are necessary. We had to learn to stay focused on the long-lasting benefits of being liberated rather than focusing on the burdensome feelings of "letting go".

Chapter Five: Walking in the Favor of God (FOG)

You anoint my head with oil; my cup overflows. Surely goodness and mercy will follow me all the days of my life, and I will dwell in the house of the LORD forever. **Psalm 25:6-7**

I recently talked to one of my close friends about our road to paying off of our debts. She said she was interested in paying off her student loans, but she didn't know where she would get the extra money to put toward the debt. My advice to anyone wanting to start down this path is to pray, set a goal, and focus your eyes on the goal. Once you are laser-focused on the goal, and as you are traveling along the way, good things and opportunities will find you.

As we were walking in faith, we were also walking in favor. God literally sent unexpected blessings our way. Everything from unexpected income to unforeseen assistance along the way. These things weren't from any of our doing. These didn't take any of our family's elbow grease. These were just straight up "favor". We had unexplained, but verified to be accurate, checks come in. Andre has received raises. Without any advertising, I had a continuous flow of clients coming to my legal practice.

One of the biggest blessings we received was my mother watching our children for us. She stepped up on a daily basis to take care of our son so that I could homeschool our other children. She served as impromptu childcare when we had client meetings. This was an invaluable blessing. It wasn't until we had surprising opportunities arise that we realized that childcare played an intricate part in this journey. We were able to put our head down and work hard because of my mother's support.

While it may not sound like one, another huge blessing we received was a denial. Early in our process, I was presented with an opportunity to partner with another lawyer. I was thrilled about the idea as it was something that I had looked forward to for a long time. However, soon after starting the venture, he backed out of the partnership. I felt crushed, but I kept reminding myself that "God knows the plans that He has for me." I also reminded myself that "What is for me is for me, what is not is not." Weeks after the partnership crumbled before my eyes, I realized what a blessing it was that it didn't get too far off of the ground. Although the venture could have been very lucrative, it would have significantly shifted my priorities. Paying off debts was a priority for us, but it wasn't our primary priority. Above paying off debts, we desired to give our children more time with me. This denial was a reminder of that and that everything needs to be done decently and in order.

God is not a respecter of persons. If He made it happen for us, he can make it happen for you too! Our debt seemed massive to us. They were mortgage size debts. We started tackling them on one income. Although some of it was us seizing opportunities, which we will talk about in the next chapter, a lot of it was faith and favor.

What We Learned

Once we got laser-focused and committed to tackling our debt, God brought blessings. Sometimes the blessings felt great, and sometimes they didn't. Either way, everything was working together for our good.

Chapter Six: Seizing Opportunities

What is the benefit, my fellow believers, if someone claims to have faith but has no works? Can that faith save him? ***James 2:14***

When a person goes bankrupt, they go through a court-mandated program where they have to pay back some or all of their debts. Sometimes they have to sell a lot of their assets in order to do so. Often times they have to stick to a strict budget in order to pay back their creditors. What we did was, essentially, a "voluntary" bankruptcy. We seized every reasonable opportunity to pay back our debts with haste.

As we stated before, when we started crushing our debt, we were a single income family. Our strategy to eliminate the debt included coming up with creative ways to bring income into our household. We actively sought out money-makers. If it sounded like it would bring in extra cash without overburdening our familial relationships, we did it. We had opportunities that worked for us, and we had opportunities that didn't. We weren't afraid to try new opportunities, and we weren't afraid to admit when something wasn't working for our family.

Twa'Lea tried her hand at in-home childcare. We thought this would be perfect for our family. Twa'Lea has a teaching credential and a graduate degree in early childhood education. She went and got her license, and had a pupil in no time. As she got her feet wet in the childcare business she quickly realized that there were aspects of the in-home childcare that proved to be challenging for her. She didn't just throw in the towel. She tried many variations of childcare, tutoring, and child entrepreneurship workshops. The business wasn't as lucrative as we had anticipated it to be, but it brought in a few coins.

Twa'Lea also took on some extra clients in her law practice. She has been practicing law for almost ten years. She practiced full-time for years, but took a hiatus after having our second child. During this season of seizing opportunities, she decided to run a lean home-based law practice. Initially, she had reservations about how people would view her professionally. She thought that clients would want to hire an attorney that had an office outside of her home. She did not let those reservations stop her. She hung her shingle in our home, consulted with clients outside of our home, and scheduled court appearances around our family calendar. Her home-based practice brought in more income than we anticipated.

I set my sights on both an old and a new venture. A few years ago I taught community college classes. I took on teaching some more classes during the second year of our journey and taught the classes in the evenings a couple of nights a week. The income was helpful in closing in on our student loan balances.

As for a new venture, I studied for and passed the real estate licensing exam and thus became a real estate agent. There was only a small upfront investment in the licensing portion, but it more than paid for itself within a couple of months of becoming an agent. We saved money on the sale of our rental property because I served as the agent on the sale. We also earned money through the sale of other real estate transactions throughout this process. Stepping out on faith for this new venture was not only pivotal in slaying our debts, but it will also prove to be very lucrative for us when we rebuild our savings

All of the new opportunities that we seized upon helped us increase our disposable income. At the onset of paying down our debts, they seemed insurmountable because our disposable income wasn't large. When we increased our disposable income, the debt started looking conquerable. However, our debt was quite large and our pay-off date of December 2020 seemed far far away. We decided to seize a few other opportunities. We decided to sell our rental property and our family home to cash in on the equity.

The decision to sell our real estate properties wasn't an easy one. In a perfect world, we would have been able to eliminate our debt at record speed, keep our rental property, and stay in our large two-story home. However, for us, we had to look at the long endgame. The sooner we stopped accruing interest on our monster loans, the sooner would could start doubling down on saving for retirement, future college tuition for our children, and getting back to enjoying the fruits of our labor. We know that God has amazing things in store for us and that includes restoring everything that we sacrificed in this season.

What We Learned

Do what you have to do to get where you want to be. If it is legal and it will help eliminate debt, be willing to consider it as an option. All too often people will put arbitrary limits on themselves and their potential. Don't block blessings. God might send someone to bless a business endeavor in a way that one ever considered possible.

Chapter Seven: The Trickle Down Effect

Train up a child in the way that he should go and when he is old he will not depart from it. ***Proverbs 22:6***

A great opportunity presented itself while we were paying off our debt. Our children are at the age where they ask for things. When I say "ask for things," I mean they ask for trips to Paris, hot air balloon rides, and trips to Disneyland. These are some of the big desires they have communicated to us. Then, there are the everyday things they ask for us to provide for them. On one hand, it makes us happy that they have lofty dreams and goals. On the other hand, while we were going through this time of extreme discipline, it pained me to know that some of the things that we were able to do with-and for-them before, we were not able to do.

In order to help them understand that we were being disciplined and paying off debt, we talked to them about borrowing and debt. We told them that our "extra money" was going toward creating a better future for all of us. We explained how we are taking steps so that they would not have to experience the bondage of debt. We talked about living within our means. However, one of the best things we did was give them an opportunity to create their own income to enjoy some of the luxuries they wanted to experience.

Our kids created their own businesses. Each of them developed business and marketing plans for their ventures. They sold their products and services to friends and family. They were required to give tithes, save a portion, and then they could spend some. They raised enough money to purchase their own tickets to Disneyland.

Their entrepreneurial efforts taught us all valuable lessons. The kids learned how to create wealth for themselves and how to be fiscally responsible. They also learned the basics principles of entrepreneurship. We learned that, even in this disciplined time, we could be creative in order to help our children have a few luxuries.

We started this journey with our children's best interests in mind and, by including them in the process, we were able to see the manifestation of benefits throughout the journey. The lessons we were learning on this life-changing journey had already begun trickling down to our children. That felt amazing. We liken the trickle down to the "overflow". God doesn't want us just to have enough for ourselves. He wants us to have an overflow. When we are so full of knowledge and wisdom, it should overflow down to our children. In the next season, we plan to be able to have wisdom, knowledge, and financial blessings, to be able to overflow on to them.

What We Learned

Our financial blessings aren't just for us. They are for our children. They are for those around us. We want to live life in the overflow.

Chapter Eight: Giving Our Way Through

Give, and it will be given to you. They will pour into your lap a good measure—pressed down, shaken together, and running over. For with the standard of measurement you use, it will be measured to you in return. ***Luke 6:38***

This journey started with a sacrificial gift of $2,500 to our home ministry. Although the concept of giving wasn't new to us, sacrificial giving would be a running theme throughout the process of slaying our debts.

I've been a 100 percent tither since I was seventeen years old. I was getting ready to make decisions about college, I was developing lofty education and career goals. This is when I was introduced to the financial promises of God. When my pastor taught on Malachi 3:10-11 it resonated in my soul. I was at a point in my life when I knew that I was going to need all the financial blessings I could get and I could not afford to be "eating my seeds."

Growing up, financial responsibility and stability was something exhibited in my home. My father was in the United States Air Force, and my mother was a jack-of-all-trades. I did not grow up with rich parents, but they were prudent with the income they brought home. Neither of my parents had credit cards nor did they have checking accounts. Layaway is how my parents purchased Christmas presents and electronics. My father practiced "envelope billing." Every first of the month, he would write down his bills on the back of an envelope and then go get money orders for them and mail them off. My dad talked to me about the importance of having good credit and emphasized not taking out "bad debt." So, when I found out that the Word stated that giving was the key to financial stability and prosperity I decided to try God at His Word. It was one of the best decisions of my life.

Andre's experience growing up was quite different than mine. His parents had different philosophical views on money. His dad worked multiple jobs but was very cavalier with his income. He looked at money as something to spend. On the other hand, his mother was a saver. She used her income to help ends meet. They had a lot of department store revolving credit cards. His mom would use math as a way to talk about money and financial principles. His mom began working in a bank when Andre was in middle school. When he got into high school they began having more in-depth conversations about money. While in college, Andre worked and gave to his church ministry when he attended church.

When Andre and I started seriously dating I was adamant about us tithing as a couple. Andre was 100 percent on board. So by the time we started attacking our debts, we had been faithfully tithing and giving as a couple for ten years. The giving we did prior to our debt elimination, and the giving we did during our snowballing felt entirely different though.

The giving during this season of our lives felt different than the giving prior to our debt elimination because after we gave, saved, and paid bills, we could usually make ourselves feel good by spending our residual income on something that brought us joy. We could buy some nice new gadget, or we could put it towards going on a nice excursion. We would work hard and get to play hard. The spending helped us feel good about being "responsible adults." Spending was our reward for "adulting."

During our season of eradicating our debt, we were working harder than we had ever worked at any other time in our lives. We were bringing more money into our home than at any other time in our lives. Despite this rise in income, we had to continue to give, and we did not get to enjoy any of the residual income. It is a humbling feeling to know that all the money you have worked hard for is going to what feels like a bottomless pit.

Our giving through this season really felt sacrificial. We didn't have a large cushion or safety net. The checks and money transfers to our church seemed larger than usual. Despite the feeling of being strapped for cash, there was this feeling of excitement to bring our tithe into the storehouse. We could see God bringing the increase. We experienced Malachi 3:10-11 up close and personal. God was our safety net. He was rebuking the devourer and we were producing more and more fruit. The joy that used to be derived from spending, started coming from our giving. Giving definitely felt better than paying large sums to the student loan company.

What We Learned

No matter what happens, just keep giving. There is true unspeakable joy in giving!

Chapter Nine: Moving at the Speed of Patience

Knowing this, that the trying of your faith worked patience. But let patience have her perfect work, that you may be perfect and entire, wanting nothing. ***James 1:3-4***.

When we first started annihilating our debt, we had great momentum. We were excited and motivated. However, our debt was large and the journey was long. There were times when it felt like we had been deprived for years on end. We watched people around us traveling. We would scroll through our social media timelines and see our friends "living their best lives." We had to turn down offers to participate in activities that we would usually engage in with family. Twa'Lea didn't get to indulge in "Black Friday" shopping. Almost all of our "new" clothes and household items came from thrift stores. Sometimes the feeling of deprivation was overwhelming.

So what did we do? One thing that helped reenergize us is attending Dave Ramsey's Smart Conference. We recommend that anyone looking to get out of debt attend a Dave Ramsey Smart Conference. You won't regret it. The energy in the room is invigorating. The information is life-changing but simple. Being in a room full of people who are all trying to escape the bondage of debt is encouraging.

I get a kick out of telling the story behind us actually getting to the conference. The conference was held in Boston, Massachusetts. We live in Sacramento, California. At the time of the conference, we were in the thick of "snowballing" our debt. We did not have any "extra" money laying around to get there. The conference itself is super affordable. The Ramsey team does a great job in helping to eliminate that barrier for people following Dave's principles. However, traveling to the conference was a different story. We ended up using the remainder of our credit card points to secure our plane tickets, hotel stay, and rental car. Oh, the irony! We had cut up those cards months before but still had access to the points, and we ended up using the final fruits of that credit card relationship to go to a conference that would motivate us to get out of debt.

The last six months of eliminating the debt were trying as well. This was about the time that we decided to put our family home on the market. I liken it to the analogy of trying to lose your last ten pounds when you're on a diet. Our debt was down to about $70,000. We could see the light at the end of the tunnel. We could smell the aroma of victory. We looked around to see what else we could do or what else we could leverage. That's when we decided to take a chance on the equity of our home. There was no way we were going to take out a home equity loan or refinance our home because we did not want to "re-categorize" the debt. We wanted the debt GONE. Selling the house revitalized us. We weren't sad about it. We didn't feel pressured to do it. We had our sights set on the finish line. We were pressing along to see what the end was going to be.

Although the journey was only twenty-four months, throughout the entire journey there needed to be a level of patience that we had to operate in. As much as we wanted the feeling of "tightness" to be over, we still had to walk the journey out and endure the struggling moments. We had to trust the process. One of Twa'Lea's former pastors - ironically it was the one who taught her the principles of tithing - used to say, "When you are going through hell, don't stop and pitch a tent, keep going!" That is what we did. We kept going. Now here we are, debt-free, and we finished paying off our debts twenty-one months ahead of schedule.

What We Learned

Trust the process. If it were easy, everyone would be living a debt-free life. Let patience have her perfect work.

Chapter Ten: Leaving Stones Behind

Go over before the ark of the LORD your God into the middle of the Jordan. Each of you is to take up a stone on his shoulder, according to the number of the tribes of the Israelites, to serve as a sign among you. In the future, when your children ask you, 'What do these stones mean?' tell them that the flow of the Jordan was cut off before the ark of the covenant of the LORD. When it crossed the Jordan, the waters of the Jordan were cut off. These stones are to be a memorial to the people of Israel forever. ***Joshua 4:5-7***

So now that we are debt free, what's next? First, we are reveling in the simple fact that we owe nothing to no one but to love them. Just to be able to say that feels pretty amazing. Next, we are setting new goals and making new plans. We will continue taking advantage of our new streams of income so that we save and invest money. Ten years ago we completed graduate school. That is where most of our student loan debt came from. In the next ten years, we will have one child graduating from high school. We are going to do everything within our power to make sure that she, and our two other children, do not go into bondage with student loans. So the financial grind for us does not end here.

We also look forward to being bigger givers! This process has given us a different perspective on giving. Now that we are debt free, we can be more flexible with giving our money and our time. Since our disposable income has increased, we have the ability to be more flexible. We want to be conduits for Christ. We can imagine a life where we give more than we consume. That is a big dream, but with God, all things are possible.

Not only do we want to help set our children up for success and be bigger givers, but we also want to help others navigate the waters of financial freedom. That is why we are writing this book. God did not bless us for us to be hoarders of the knowledge that we gained. He blessed us to share our experience. That is what we will do. We will help guide and encourage others that are traveling the path we traveled, and we will tell everyone within earshot how good and faithful God is.

God was the leader of this journey. He started the good work in us and He is faithful to complete it. Our way and method was in no means the ONLY way to slay debt. Some people thought "it didn't take all that," or that what we were doing was extreme. Our way worked though. Also, we should add that we did not create the blueprint we used to get out of debt. We yielded to wise counsel, humbled ourselves, stepped out on faith, and put in some elbow grease. We made tough decisions. We followed through. We didn't quit. Really and truly, anyone can slay their debt.

What We Learned

Anyone can do what we did. Some people will just need to hear that it is possible.

Chapter Eleven: The Recap

The Overview of What We Did

1. **We got fed up with our debt.** We wanted to see it off of our budget sheet, and we wanted financial security for our family.

2. **We read Dave Ramsey's *The Total Money Makeover.*** He does an amazing job of detailing the importance of financial freedom. He also shares stories of other people who have successfully delivered themselves from debt. After reading this book we had a clear roadmap to what needed to be done to get rid of our debt and live the type of life we envisioned. We recommend that anyone thinking of eliminating debt, start by reading this book.

3. We aligned ourselves with our home church's giving campaign and **gave a sacrificial offering.** The key to any successful life includes giving. The Bible talks about giving intensely. Giving not only helps the receiver, but giving also releases blessings for the giver. We knew we needed all the blessings we could get.

4. **We put our plan into action.** We revised our budget to redirect all disposable income to go toward student loans. If it wasn't a bill, gas, or food for our house, it was crossed off our budget. We also took all of our savings and put it toward our debt. We ran a "lean, mean, no extra spending machine." This took discipline and sacrifice, but we knew it would pay off in the end.

5. **We held an expectation that God was going to bring the increase.** This was a walk of faith. Many blessings

came our way along this journey. Some blessings came in the form of denial. We made peace with denials and embraced help from those around us.

6. **We put in work.** We did not just sit and wait for money to fall in our laps. We actively sought out ways to create new streams of income. If it was legal, we tried it. If it didn't work for our family, we discontinued it. Earning money wasn't the primary goal. A better life for our family was. If making money wasn't in alignment with that, then it quickly discontinued it.

7. **We included our children.** We used our journey as a way to teach our children about financial freedom. We helped them create their own entrepreneurial ventures, and we let them pay for their own trip to Disneyland.

8. **We kept giving.** Even though we were directing funds towards paying off debts, we stayed faithful to our tithe. We see our tithe as seed and we didn't want to eat our seed. Giving through our deprivation began to bring an unspeakable joy.

9. **We let patience have her perfect work.** There were times when we felt like we were going through a drought at a snail's speed. During those times we took steps to invigorate ourselves without breaking the bank. We also took drastic measures when necessary to jump-start a new pace.

10. **We are leaving stones behind to memorialize this journey.** We never want to forget how we bunkered down and did what needed to be done. Our plan is to share the knowledge of how we conquered our debt with anyone

who will listen. We also plan to encourage others who are seeking to break free from the bondage of debt.

About the Author

Twa'Lea Jordan, is a modern-day Renaissance woman and advocate. She is an attorney, a credentialed educator, self-published author, entrepreneur, military combat-veteran, and community activist. She is a wife, and a mother of three dynamic children. In her spare time, Twa'Lea enjoys cooking and traveling the world.

Andre O. Jordan, a Boston-born native, is a loving husband and father. He has worked in the financial services industry for over 17 years. However, he is also an Adjunct Professor of Business and Economics, a Realtor ®, public speaker and he actively serves as an Officer in the United States Air Force Reserves. He is a believer that all things are possible through faith in God's Word, hard work, and commitment. He enjoys working out, motorcycling, traveling and eating Twa'Lea's gourmet cuisines.

Made in United States
Troutdale, OR
11/03/2026

56845096R00021